Snowflakes from Heaven

To Carson
Best Wishes!
Jeff Yosick

by Jeff Yosick & illustrated by Phyllis Stewart

Copyright

Snowflakes from Heaven ISBN 1440455910
EAN-13   9781440455919
www.narrowpathbooks.com
www.jyosick.com

Cover Design, illustrations and layout by Phyllis Stewart
Phyllis can be contacted at
pstewart0831@sbcglobal.net

Printed in the USA

NARROW PATH
PUBLICATIONS

Based on a true story.

It was a very cold day in early December. A young boy named Eric was bundled up in his wheelchair next to his mother and father. They had made a special trip to Eric's favorite place, Hayden's Park, to experience the first snow of the season together.

Eric sat quietly with his eyes closed and head tilted toward the sky. As a gentle breeze brushed across his face, he opened his mouth to catch a snowflake. After a few moments of waiting, he felt a sudden cool tingle on the top of his tongue.

Immediately bursting into a grin he exclaimed, "I caught one!" Eric's parents smiled. It didn't take long before they also joined in on the fun. The three of them spent the next several minutes doing their best to catch snowflakes. When they finally grew tired and decided to stop, they counted a total of eleven snowflakes that they'd caught together.

"Wow!" said Eric's father, "Eleven snowflakes!"

"I wonder if it's a new record!" replied Eric.

Eric's mother wrapped her arms around him and snuggled up close to him. As she leaned her head next to his, she began to wonder if this would be Eric's last Christmas. He was only seven and had been sick for most of his life. Eric suffered from a disease that couldn't be fixed by medicine or doctors. He had a brother named Bobby that had died from the same disease just one year before. Like Bobby, Eric was also dying. It made moments like this special day at the park even more precious for his parents.

After feeling the warmth of his mother next to him, Eric reached his hands toward the falling snow, "Do you think there are snowflakes in heaven?"

There was a brief pause before his mother answered, "Yes, honey, I do. I believe that snowflakes actually begin in heaven and then fall straight to earth."

"Why?" asked Eric.

"Because snowflakes are one of the many things that God uses to give us a glimpse of how beautiful heaven will be," replied his father.

Eric smiled, "Will we be able to catch snowflakes on our tongues?"

"We sure will, Honey, we sure will," replied his mother as she held back her tears.

The rest of their time at Hayden's Park was spent exploring the many different paved trails. Eric had always enjoyed nature, especially at the park. There were deer, bunnies, squirrels, and many types of birds. He loved every part of that wonderful place.

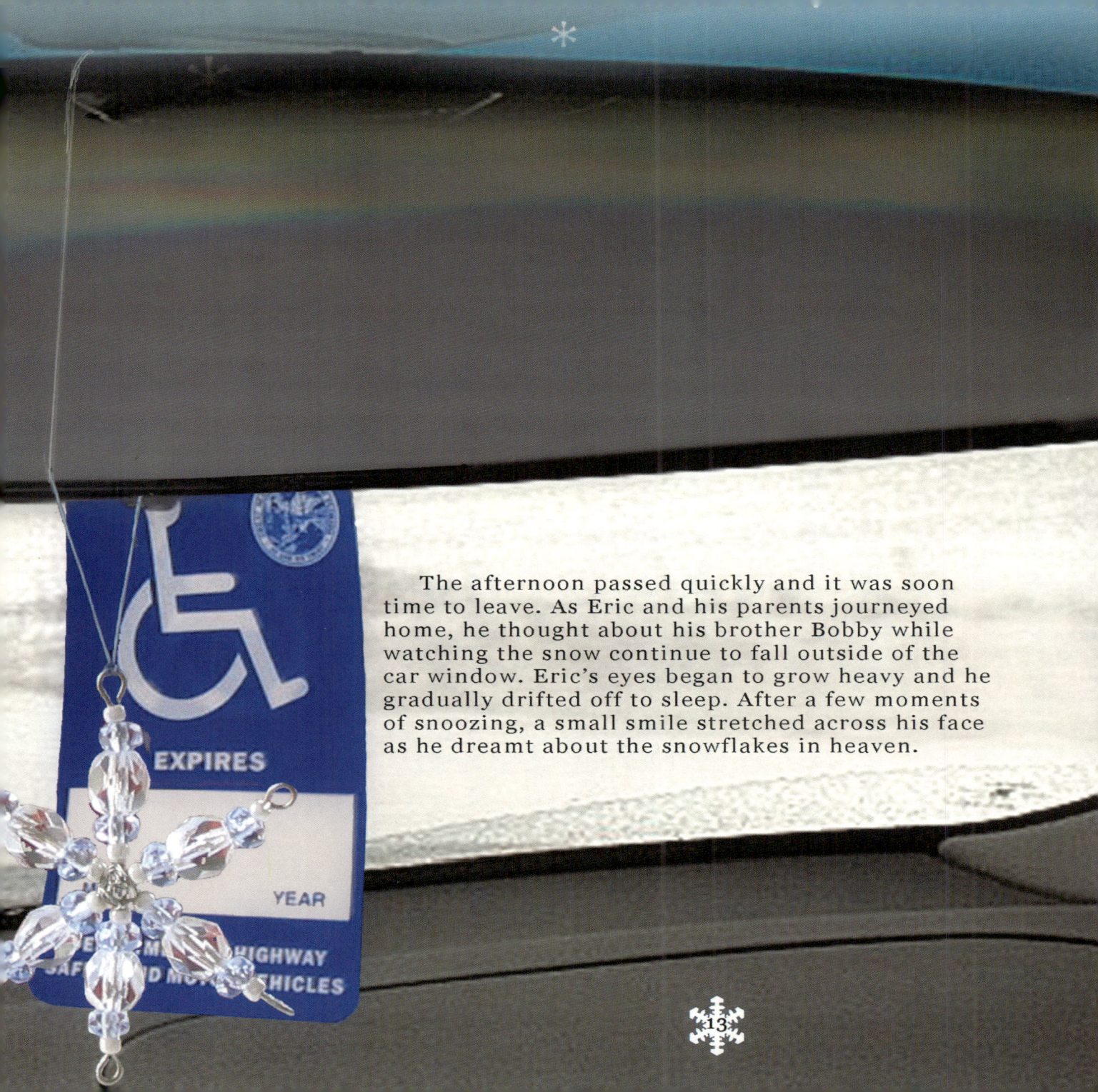

The afternoon passed quickly and it was soon time to leave. As Eric and his parents journeyed home, he thought about his brother Bobby while watching the snow continue to fall outside of the car window. Eric's eyes began to grow heavy and he gradually drifted off to sleep. After a few moments of snoozing, a small smile stretched across his face as he dreamt about the snowflakes in heaven.

The next week passed quickly and Christmas day was rapidly approaching. Eric and his family were busy with the preparations. Time was spent decorating the tree, baking cookies, and wrapping gifts. They also hung lights along the bushes at the front of the house and put a large wreath on the door. Everything looked beautiful.

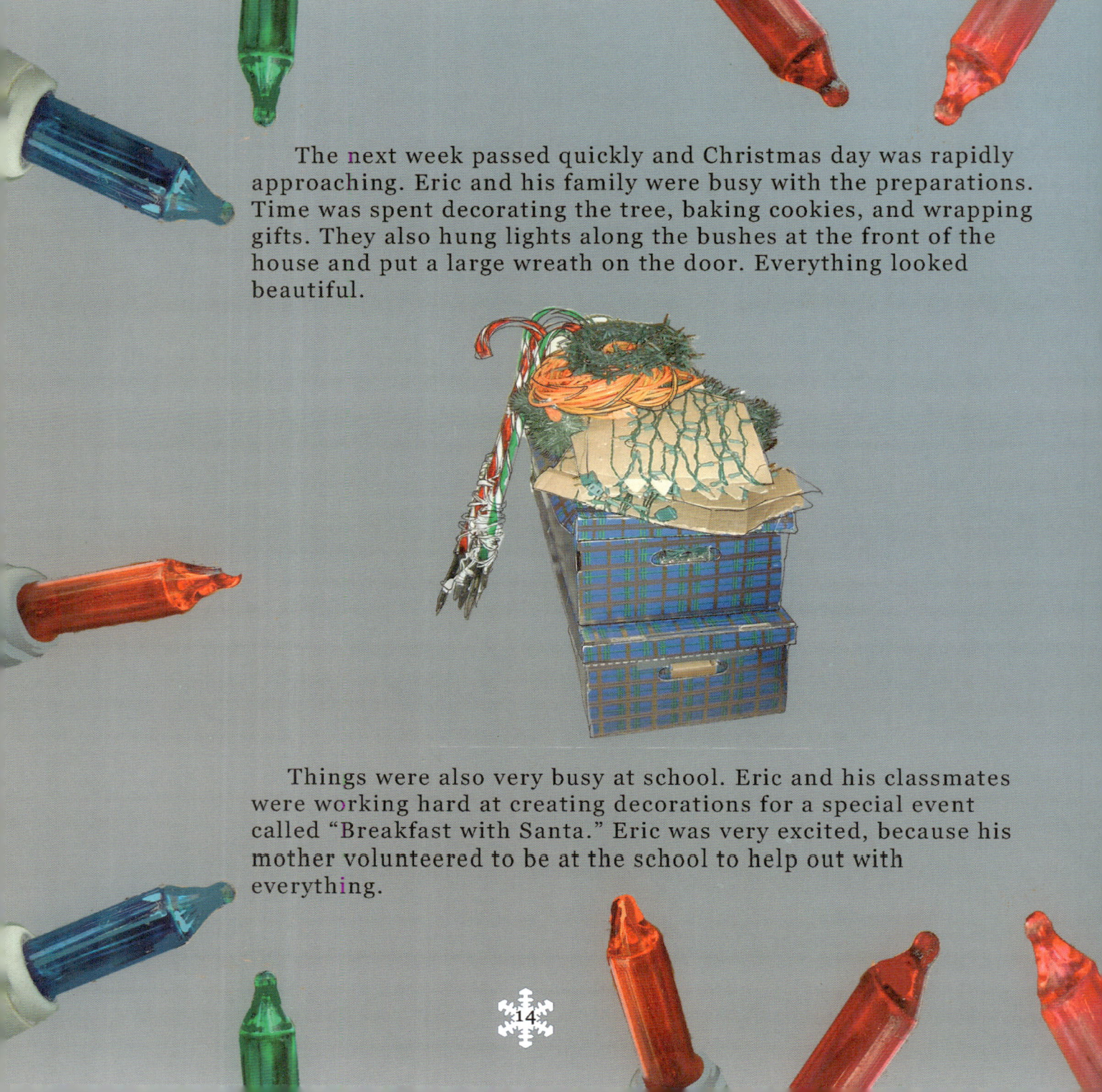

Things were also very busy at school. Eric and his classmates were working hard at creating decorations for a special event called "Breakfast with Santa." Eric was very excited, because his mother volunteered to be at the school to help out with everything.

After a week of preparing and eager waiting, "Breakfast with Santa" was only a day away. As Eric's mother tucked him into bed that evening, she noticed that he was unusually quiet.

"Is everything alright, Eric?" she asked. "You seem quiet tonight."

"I think so," he replied with some hesitation.

"What's the matter, Honey?"

"Well, I just found out today about a boy that goes to school in another building. He has been really sick just like me. I don't really know him, but I'm worried about him."

"Your teacher told me about him a couple of weeks ago. His name is Jonathan, and he is in the second grade." Eric's mother leaned over to give him a hug and noticed tears streaming from his eyes.

"Is Jonathan going to die like Bobby and me?" he asked.

"I don't know, Honey," she replied, "I just don't know."

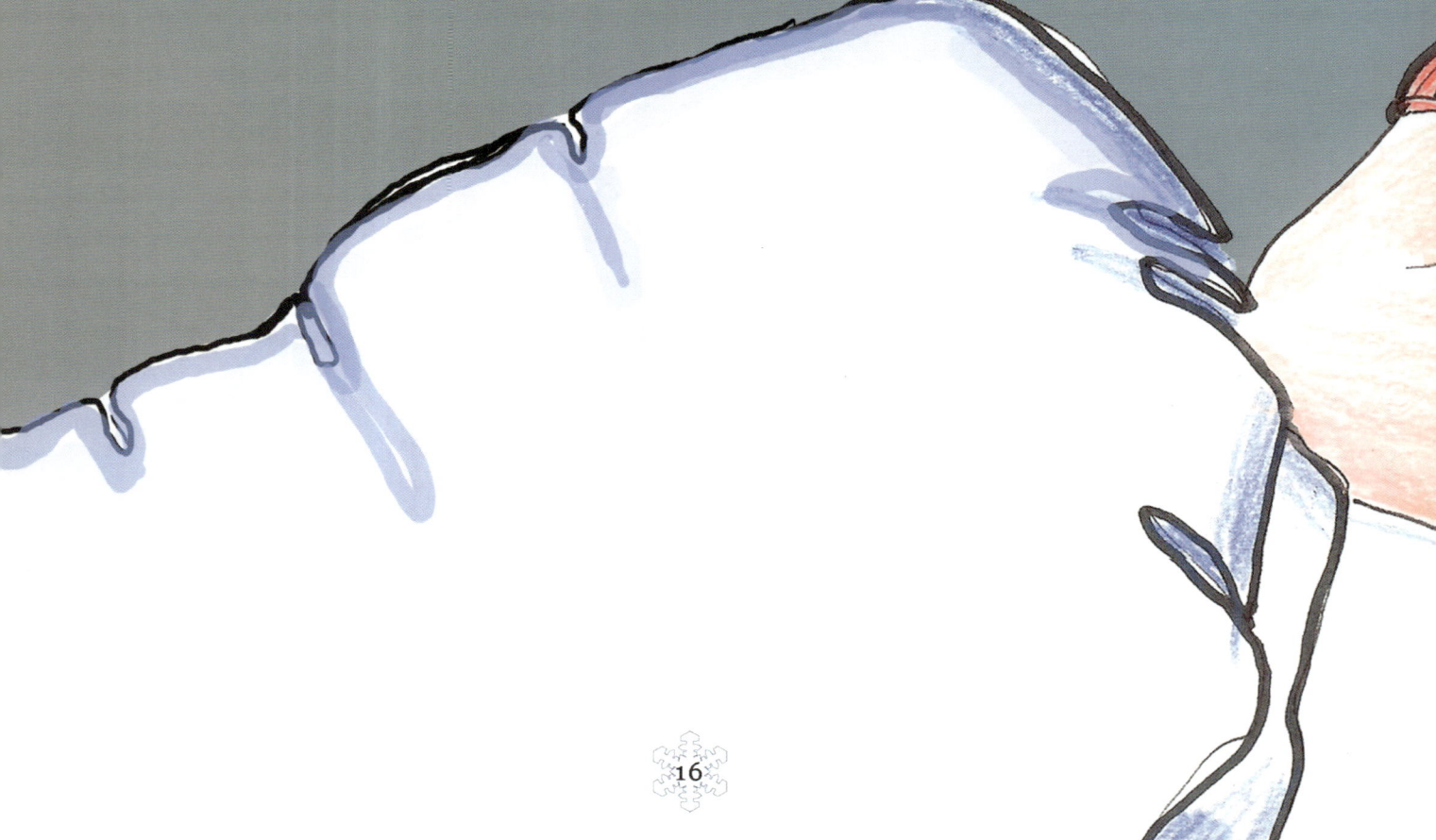

The next morning, Eric and his mother arrived early at the school and everything was ready to go. The cafeteria was decorated for Santa's arrival, and the delicious smell of breakfast cooking had filled the entire school.

Eric sat quietly in his wheelchair watching his classmates and other children from his school arriving for the special morning. It wasn't long before everyone began to form a line for breakfast.

Eric's attention was soon turned away from the crowd of people and toward the sound of his mother's voice, "Are you hungry Eric?"

He looked up to see his mother standing with two trays of food. They looked delicious! Eric's mother had picked out pancakes and juice for him. They were his favorite.

"Oh great, pancakes!" he remarked as she handed him the tray. "Mom, do you remember how much Bobby loved pancakes?"

"I sure do."

Eric paused, "I wish he could have been here today."

With a tremble in her voice she replied, "Bobby would have loved this."

Eric and his mother enjoyed the wonderful breakfast together. They shared a few laughs and memories of Bobby before discussing some of the exciting things they would be doing for Christmas. Eric was trying his best to finish his last pancake, when the main door to the cafeteria opened and Santa walked in.

"Ho, Ho, Ho, Merry Christmas!" chuckled Santa.

Children began to shuffle nervously in their seats as he walked toward the front of the room. Smiles and giggles of excitement filled the air as they all watched in wonder. Tiny whispers could be heard between the children discussing what they would say when it became their turn to sit on Santa's lap.

When he reached the front of the room, Santa took his place in the chair that was prepared for him. The children then began to slowly line up for a chance to visit him. As Eric's mother pushed his wheelchair over to the line she couldn't help but wonder if this would be the last time he would ever sit on Santa's lap.

The time spent in line went quick and it was soon Eric's turn to visit with Santa. Eric's mother moved the wheelchair next to Santa, and then helped him climb onto his lap.

"Well, hello there young man. What's your name?" asked Santa.

"Eric," he replied.

"What would you like for Christmas, Eric?"

After a few brief moments Eric looked up at Santa and began to speak in a slow soft voice. "Well, you see Santa, I've been sick for a long time. I had a brother named Bobby that died a year ago from the same thing I have. It's something that the doctors can't fix and I'm probably not going to live much longer. I'm not afraid of dying. Heaven is going to be wonderful place and I'll get to be with Bobby again. I'm just sad that I won't have the chance to make a difference in the world. Santa, the greatest gift I could get for Christmas is just one chance to make a difference for someone."

Santa paused for a moment as a tear trickled down his cheek, "What do you have in mind, Eric?"

Eric leaned over and whispered into Santa's ear. Upon hearing what he had shared, Santa smiled and gave him a big hug. He then handed Eric two candy canes and gave him a wink. His mother was there waiting and helped him back into the wheelchair. She then pushed Eric over to the side of the room.

"Eric, I need to help clean things up in the kitchen. Are you going to be alright to wait here?" she asked.

"I'll be fine, Mom," he replied.

One by one the children continued to visit with Santa. The minutes passed by and something interesting began to happen. Eric began to wiggle out of his wheelchair and make his way over to where Santa was sitting. In fact, he did it several times. On each trip Santa would give him a couple candy canes. After many visits, Eric's seat was full of candy canes.

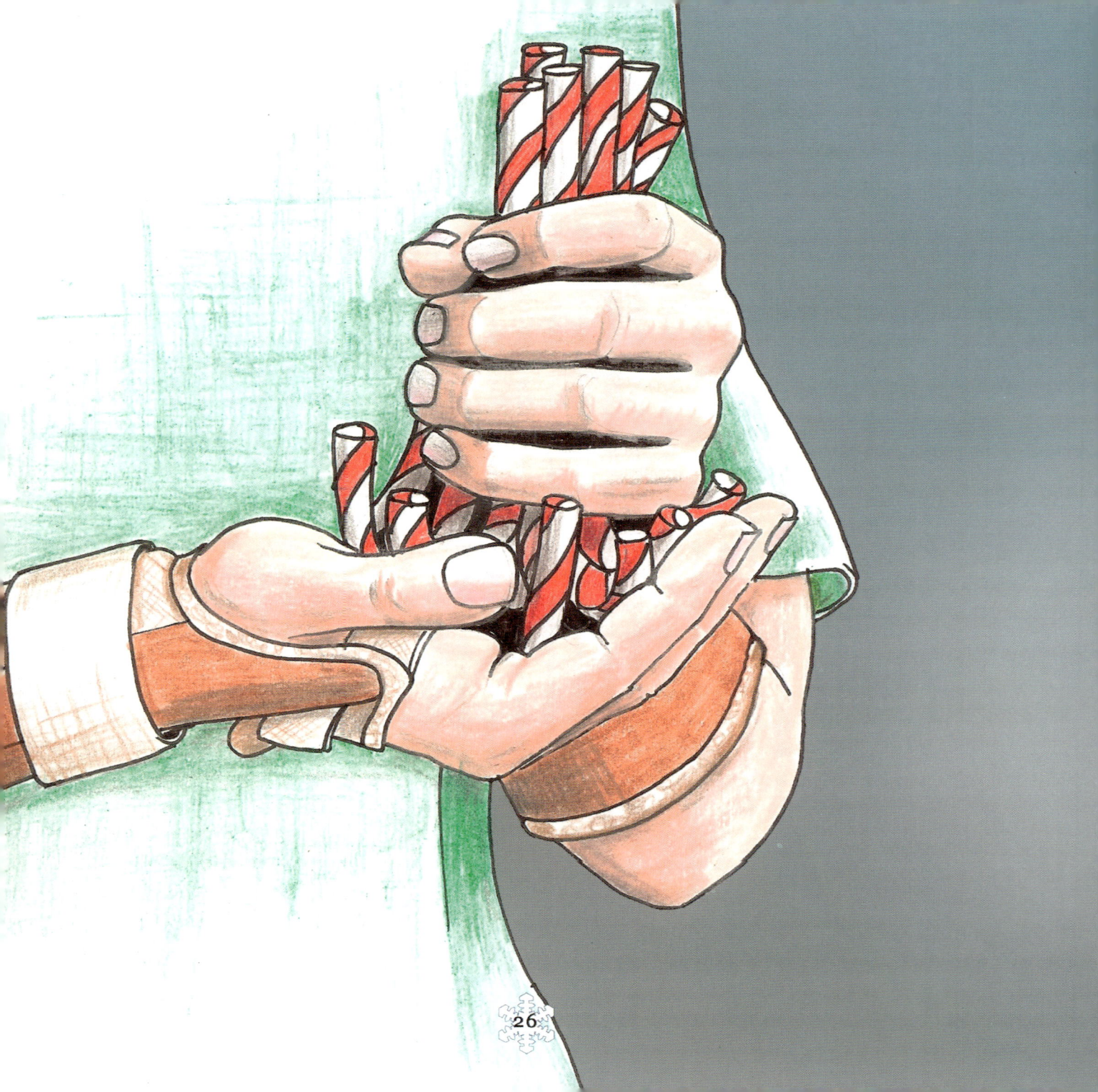

People began to notice what Eric was doing and a couple of his classmates walked over to where he was sitting.

"Why are you collecting all of those candy canes?" asked his friend, Michael.

Eric replied, "I'm going to sell them to raise money for a boy who is very sick."

"What's his name?" asked his other friend, Sophie.

"His name is Jonathan, and he goes to school in the other building."

"How much are they?" asked Michael.

"They're one dollar," he replied.

Sophie and Michael looked at each other before running over to their parents to explain to them what Eric was doing. It wasn't long before they both returned with money to buy a few of the candy canes.

Soon, word spread and more children and parents began to file over to purchase candy canes. Some of the people were buying two and three at a time. At one point, Eric was beginning to run out of the candy canes. Santa saw what was happening and dumped another pile of them onto his lap.

The whole time that this wonderful moment was taking place, Eric's mother was busy working in the kitchen. A close friend of her's had just bought one of the candy canes and walked over to the kitchen to tell her about the great thing that was happening. When Eric's mother heard the news she rushed out to see him.

As she approached, Eric had just sold his last candy cane. He sat quietly for a few seconds while looking at the pile of money he had collected for Jonathan. Then he slowly looked up at his mother and smiled.

"I wanted to do something special, Mom, something for Jonathan."

"I'm so proud of you!" replied his mother as her eyes filled with tears. She knelt down next to his chair and held him close to her. Her thoughts soon raced back to the first time she ever held him and how hard it would be to have to let him go.

"You're an angel, Eric, you're truly an angel," she whispered.

The "Breakfast with Santa" event came to a close and everyone began filing toward the door to leave. Eric's mother stayed behind to help clean things up. When it was finished she walked over to where Eric was waiting.

"Are you ready to go?" she asked.

"I'm ready if you are!" he replied with a smile.

As Eric's mother pushed him out of the school, beautiful snowflakes began to gently fall from the sky.

Eric quickly noticed them and smiled, "Look, Mom, it's snowing." She returned a smile of her own and together they caught more snowflakes from heaven.

The Krenzke Family, 1995

In Memory of the Krenzke Family
Lind, Pam, Eric and Bobby

I, Eric and Bobby's Grandmother, have been asked to write and explain why the Krenzke family was so special. I feel that it was their faith and their love for each other and their fellow man that set them apart.

Pam and Lind met at Ball State University in 1981. In May 1983 they married and moved to Muncie, Indiana, and then on to Columbus, Ohio where Lind took a job with Compuserve. Pam worked for the State Department.

In mid December 1984, we received flowers from Pam and Lind with a card which read, "Did you know a baby is magic?" (Lind did magic as a hobby.) That's how we found out that Robert Carl Krenzke was going to be born. I don't believe I've ever seen two people more excited about having a baby. Lind did not want the unborn baby to be called "it", so they called him "Eggroll". Bobby was born on August 6th, 1985. He was a good-looking baby with a full head of hair and was well loved. Bobby talked in full sentences by the time he was a year and a half old. He was a loving boy and loved to be read to and listen to stories.

On January, 30th 1989, Bobby's brother Eric Michael Krenzke was born. Eric was a beautiful baby, too. Pam and I had the boys at the mall when Eric was about 6 weeks old and a lady came up to me and asked if the baby was a boy or girl. When I said, "He's a boy", she replied, "Well, he's pretty enough to be a girl!"

Early in his life Eric was diagnosed with a disease called Dystonia, a hereditary neurological movement disorder characterized by involuntary muscle contractions. We were devastated to find that it was a disease without a cure, but Eric's parents treated him just like Bobby, and the brothers loved each other very much.

This disease caused Eric to fall frequently and he had many broken bones. He had to wear a helmet to prevent head injuries. Once, when Eric had a broken arm, Bobby put on one of Eric's extra helmets and wrapped his arm up so they would look alike.

We were all shocked when Bobby was diagnosed with the same disease as his little brother. Pam said, "This is a parent's worse nightmare." Bobby always wanted to make a difference in the world, as he had seen his parents do many times in helping others. Sadly, Bobby died on May 16, 1995 when he was nine years old.

One way that Pam, who was working for the Columbus School System, found to help cope with Bobby's loss was to start a line of books to support the purchase of program materials including reading books, coloring books and puppets to help children in hospice support groups safely explore their feelings. They called the program "Bobby's Books".

Pam and Lind had been working on adopting another child before Bobby got sick. So, on February 12, 1996 Betsy came into our lives. Eric was delighted with her. Once someone remarked, "It's a shame Bobby can't see her." Eric, in his seven year old wisdom replied, "Don't you know Bobby picked her out in heaven and sent her to us?" Even at their young ages the boys always knew they would go to heaven. Eric also loved the fact that he had a chance to be a younger brother, an only child, and a big brother. He said that he didn't think too many people could say that. In August 1997, at the age of seven, Eric went to heaven to be with Bobby.

Four years later, in 2001, the Lord decided that he needed Lind, too. Lind, only 38, died unexpectedly of heart complications. Pam, of course, was devastated, as we all were. Lind was such a kind, loving and fun man. The world was just not a great place without Lind in it. It was a struggle for Pam, but she managed to raise Betsy as she had raised the boys, letting her know how much she was loved.

Sadly, in 2004, Pam, too, was diagnosed with Dystonia. She struggled with the disease for two years while continuing to raise Betsy. Before Pam died she made sure Betsy was adopted by a good Christian family. To Pam, the bottom line was, "They're in church every Sunday, and I like the way their kids have turned out." Brad and Faith Rechel and their three daughters took Betsy into their lives and into their hearts.

All of the Krenzke's made a difference in this world.

- written by Lois Kay Hinderer, Grandmother
August 2008

Bobby's Books

Using Books to Help Kids Cope

Childhood is a wonderful time. A child embraces the joy of each day. Sometimes though, sadness, fear, illness and loss enter a child's life. If you know a child who had to make such a journey, would you know how to help?

One way is to use children's books to help kids deal with difficult issues. Using children's literature as a springboard for conversations will give kids the chance to express their feelings and tell their own stories.

It is also important that children have access to a variety of books that show a broad range of emotions and feelings. This helps kids see that they can act independently, assume responsibility for their actions, tolerate frustration, approach new challenges with enthusiasm, and be proud of their accomplishments.

Use books that help kids feel good about themselves. Use a book and conversation to help a child deal with a change in routine or the death of a pet. Use everyday happenings to build a child's coping skills. You and the child will both benefit.

Bobby's Books was created and developed by Pam Krenzke. Pam was a mother, a friend, a trainer, a volunteer, and an educator. It was the loss of Pam's two sons, Bobby and Eric, due to a genetic disorder that fueled her compassion and her fire to improve one's journey through life. She was determined to make certain that parents, educators, and caregivers of children would have a resource to help children deal with their loss and grief.

Bobby Krenzke loved words, ideas, laughing and learning. He was born on August 6, 1985 and died on May 16, 1995. Bobby's Books was created in his memory and to fulfill his wish to make a difference in the world. Since Pam's death in 2006, Bobby's Books has come under the direction of Ohio Hospice & Palliative Care Organization (OHPCO). It is OHPCO's intent to honor Pam's family and her legacy by continuing to nurture and grow this special program.

Keep reading. Keep talking. Keep healing.

For more information about Bobby's Books and to learn how to help make a difference in the world, please contact

Ohio Hospice & Palliative Care Organization
555 Metro Place North, Suite 650
Dublin, Ohio 43017
Phone: (614) 763-0036
Fax: (614) 763-0050
Email: info@ohpco.org

Other Titles by Jeff Yosick

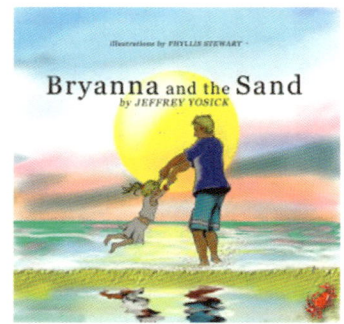

Bryanna and the Sand
illustrated by
Phyllis Stewart

A father-daughter walk and talk
on the beach, learning about life and seashells

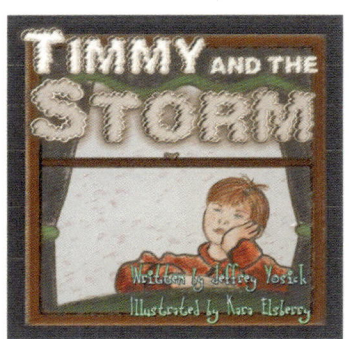

Timmy and the Storm
illustrated by
Kara Elsberry

A story to comfort the children of
military parents during times of separation

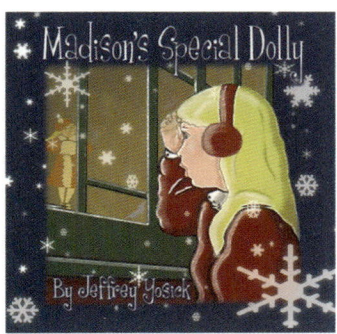

Madison's Special Doll
illustrated by
Kara Elsberry

A little girl makes a sacrifice to
brighten someone's day

Running the Race
illustrated by
Phyllis Stewart

A family deals with a close family member with cancer by finding ways to help.

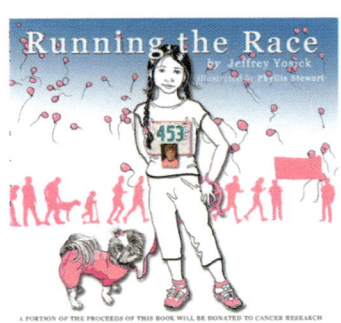

One Penney, One Hope
illustrated by
Phyllis Stewart

*A family learns ways to share.
Available Soon.*

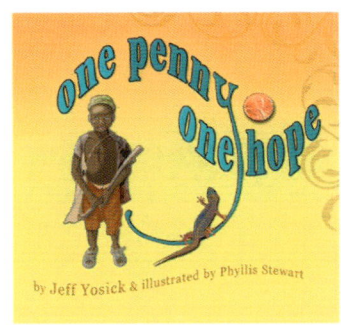

Available at

www.narrowpathbooks.com

www.amazon.com

www.jyosick.com

NARROW PATH
PUBLICATIONS

2303612

Made in the USA